City States

Inside
ANCIENT
GREECE

City
States

ANNE WRIGHT

Sharpe Focus
an imprint of M.E. Sharpe, Inc.

First edition for the United States, its territories and dependencies,
Canada, Mexico, and Australia, published in 2008 by M.E. Sharpe, Inc

Sharpe Focus
An imprint of M.E. Sharpe, Inc.
80 Business Park Drive
Armonk, NY 10504

www.mesharpe.com

Library of Congress Cataloging-in-Publication Data

Wright, Anne Margaret.
  City states / Anne Wright.
    p. cm. -- (Inside ancient Greece)
  Includes bibliographical references and index.
  ISBN 978-0-7656-8129-4 (hardcover : alk. paper)
  1. Greece--Social conditions--To 146 B.C.--Juvenile literature. 2.
Greece--Politics and government--To 146 B.C.--Juvenile literature. I.
Title.

HN10.G7W75 2008
938--dc22
                         2007011421

Editorial and design by Amber Books Ltd
Project Editor: James Bennett
Copy Editor: Deborah Murrell
Picture Research: Kate Green
Design: Andrew Easton

Cover Design: Jesse Sanchez, M.E. Sharpe, Inc.

Printed in Malaysia

9 8 7 6 5 4 3 2 1

For my mother, Dr. Margaret Robson Wright, with love.

PICTURE CREDITS

AKG-Images: 6–7, 12, 15, 18, 29, 31, 36, 38, 39, 42, 43, 44, 45, 47, 50, 52, 59, 60, 61, 64, 66, 68,
69, 71, 72, 74, 75
Corbis: 26
De Agostini: 8, 11, 13, 16–17, 20, 21, 22, 23, 24, 27, 32–33, 34–35, 41, 49, 54, 63, 73
Getty Images: 30
Mary Evans Picture Library: 46, 56

ABOUT THE AUTHOR

Anne Wright gained a First Class Honours degree from the University of St. Andrews, Scotland,
before moving on to further study at Corpus Christi College, University of Oxford. After teaching in
London, she moved back to Oxford, where she is currently Head of Classics at Summer Fields, an
independent boys' boarding school. She lives in Oxford, U.K.

Contents

Introduction   6

Chapter One   Government   8

Chapter Two   Trade and Commerce   18

Chapter Three   Pastimes and Ceremonies   24

Chapter Four   Childhood and Education   36

Chapter Five   Women and Domestic Life   50

Chapter Six   Slavery   64

Glossary   76
Glossary of Names   77
Learn More About   78
Index   79

Introduction

The civilization of the ancient Greeks has influenced the world for thousands of years. Much of what we take for granted today, in areas such as science, mathematics, drama, poetry, and philosophy, was invented by the ancient Greeks. In many other fields, too, the Greeks made huge advances in human knowledge. Modern politicians still look for inspiration to fifth-century B.C.E. Athens, the cradle of democracy. Ancient Greek plays are still performed today, and in all the major cities of the world you can find buildings heavily influenced by Greek architecture. This series of books explores the full richness of Greek culture and history. It also considers how Greek civilization still influences us today.

City States

Life in ancient Greece was different from life in the modern world in many ways. Women had few rights. They were not expected to have jobs or to meet men who were not part of their immediate family. Slavery was common and people captured in wars were often sold as slaves. Some worked as domestic servants, but others endured much harder conditions, working underground in the Athenian silver mines. This book considers all these aspects of life in ancient Greece. It also explains how Greek children were educated and sets out the various jobs that ancient Greeks did and the pleasures and pastimes which they enjoyed.

City States also looks at how the ancient Greeks still influence us today. Much Greek food from the ancient world is still enjoyed around the world.

This map shows how the Greek civilization spread across the Mediterranean Sea. It also shows important places in the Greek world, such as Olympia, where the Olympic games were held.

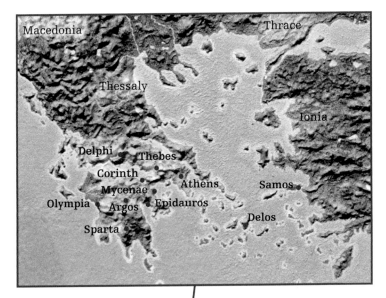

The Olympic Games are still held every four years. However, perhaps the most important Greek idea influencing us concerns government. Today, many people believe in democracy, the idea of people taking part in running their own country. Democracy was invented by the Athenians and allowed every Athenian citizen to have a say in how the state was managed. This idea has since spread throughout the world.

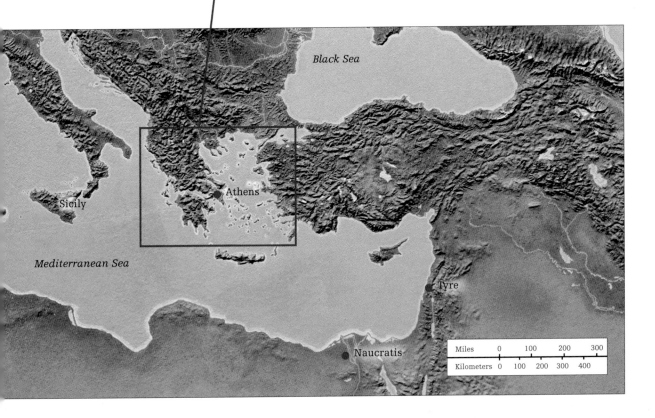

7

Polycrates and the Ring

One of the most successful Greek tyrants was Polycrates (*Puh-LICK-ruh-teez*), who ruled the island of Samos, in the Aegean Sea, from around 546 to 522 B.C.E. Under his rule, Samos enjoyed its period of greatest power and wealth. At this period, Samos not only had considerable influence in the Aegean Sea, but also had close links with the rulers of Egypt.

The historian Herodotus records that Polycrates' authority grew so great that Amasis (*Uh-MA-siss*), the pharaoh of Egypt, advised him to throw away his most precious possession. Amasis claimed that, if Polycrates did this, the gods would not punish him for having so much good fortune. Amasis may have meant that Polycrates ought to shed some of his power, but instead Polycrates chose to throw away a ring that was one of his most prized possessions. The ring was hurled far out to sea and Polycrates thought that he had now saved himself from any misfortune that the gods could send.

However, several days later a poor fisherman came to present the tyrant with a particularly fine fish he had caught. When the fish was cut open, inside its gut lay the ring. Then servants brought the ring to Polycrates, rejoicing that it had been recovered. However, Polycrates did not celebrate his good fortune, for he realized that he could not escape the fate that the gods had planned for him. Sure enough, first Amasis became less friendly, and then some men who had been exiled from Samos gained the help of the Spartans and attacked Polycrates. Polycrates defeated them, but he did not enjoy his success for long. The Persian ruler of Sardis (in modern Turkey) lured Polycrates to his city and there had him crucified before he could grow even more powerful.

The tyrant Polycrates brought the island of Samos to the height of its power and influence, and forged links with other states outside Greece, including Egypt.

Harmodius and Aristogeiton were praised by later Greeks for having rid Athens of tyranny. However, Pisistratus, the first Athenian tyrant, provided a period of stability that enabled Athens to grow more prosperous.

The ruins of the city-state of Sparta today. Sparta was much more powerful than these ruins might suggest. Unlike Athens, Sparta did not spend large sums of money creating a beautiful city.

Most oligarchies gave some political power to certain privileged groups. Spartan citizens had obvious advantages compared to less powerful members of their society. However, while throughout ancient Greece individual citizens might own slaves, Sparta was unusual in using state-owned slaves to ensure that she could develop a professional army.

Sparta also had some other unique aspects. Most oligarchies were set up when small groups of men seized power from kings or aristocrats. Instead of altogether abolishing kings, Sparta absorbed them into her political set-up. Even more unusual, at any one time, Sparta had two kings. This was because there were two royal families, each providing a king. Although this system had some benefits (for example, one king could lead the army while the other remained at home), it also led to tensions, with rivalry as to which king would have the greater influence politically.

As well as her two kings, Sparta also had five magistrates, called *Ephors* (*EFF-orz*), who were elected each year. In addition, there was an advisory council of elders, known as the

Pisistratus

Tyrants were found throughout the Greek world in the seventh and sixth centuries B.C.E. Although they were not chosen by the people they governed, tyrants often provided a period of stability. For example, Pisistratus (*Py-SIS-trah-tuss*) became the tyrant of Athens in 546 B.C.E. Before him, rival factions of Athenian aristocrats had squabbled over who was going to have power. However, once Pisistratus' rule was firmly established, he helped Athens to become more prosperous. He avoided wars and encouraged farming and trade. He provided law courts and ensured that the laws were enforced more fairly than before. Pisistratus died in 527 B.C.E. and was succeeded by his son, Hippias. However, Hippias was overthrown in 510 B.C.E. and changes were then made to the political structure to encourage power to be shared among the people of Athens.

Gerousia (*Geh-ROO-zee-uh*). The twenty-eight members of this council had to be at least 60 years old. Once elected, a councilor remained part of the Gerousia until he died. These groups provided political leadership and guidance, although a full assembly of citizens could also be called to make decisions concerning war and peace.

The government of Athens was very different from that of Sparta. There were three main parts to Athenian democracy, the *boule* (*BOO-lay*), or council, the *ecclesia* (*eh-KLAY-zee-uh*), or assembly, and the *dikasteria* (*di-kuh-STEER-ee-uh*), or law courts. The boule consisted of 500 men who drew up matters for discussion in the ecclesia. The members of the boule were selected by a lottery, so there was no possibility of one political group unfairly dominating the council.

The ecclesia consisted of all the Athenian citizens who wished to vote. Some citizens regularly attended, but some, such as those who lived a long way from the city center, would come less frequently. The ecclesia was held in the open air and could be a very boisterous place, particularly given that there could be over 6,000 people listening to the speeches. Although there were no political parties as such, different people were known to support different issues, and tempers could run very high during a debate.

The law courts were where ordinary court cases took place, and where matters concerning politics were discussed. Political matters normally consisted of a man being prosecuted for having proposed a law to which someone else objected. Voting was carried out in secret, and penalties ranged from fines to the loss of citizen rights or death.

The Athenian Empire

In the fifth century B.C.E., Athens reached the height of her power. The Persians invaded Greece and were defeated in 479 B.C.E. Athens had been closely involved in the fighting and soon after

"Magna Graecia"— Great Greece

The ancient Greeks did not just live in Greece. There were also many Greek colonies throughout the Black Sea region, France (the port of Marseilles was a Greek settlement), Spain, Egypt, North Africa, Italy, and Sicily. The colonies in Italy and Sicily were particularly numerous, and the culture of the region was heavily influenced by Greek settlers. This is why the later Romans called the area Magna Graecia, which meant "Great Greece."

These Greeks had been driven abroad by the comparative poverty of their land. It was impossible to support the growing Greek population by farming alone, so some Greek states decided to export their surplus population to different areas. These colonies often had close links with their mother city and trade was stimulated between the various regions.

the end of the Persian Wars the city had been given the leadership of the Delian League. The Delian League was an organization that had been set up to ensure the safety of the Greek states, and to punish the Persians for having invaded Greece. Its headquarters were on the island of Delos, although they later moved to Athens. Many members of the league provided money to finance a navy to protect the seas, but Athens did not pay cash. Instead, she provided ships. It was not long before Athens had the most powerful navy in the region, and soon the Delian League became a league in name only. In reality, it had become the Athenian Empire. Athens drew great wealth from her empire, much of which was spent beautifying the city. From Athens, the empire, in return, received protection from the Persians and freedom from piracy. However, the member states also increasingly lost their political independence.

Ostracism

Every year, the ecclesia was given the chance of a special vote, known as an ostracism. In an ostracism, the ecclesia selected a man to be sent into exile for ten years. The procedure was used to stop excessive quarreling between two sets of leaders, by giving the assembly the chance to get rid of one of them (although he did not lose his property or citizenship). At least 6,000 voters had to be present, and each person wrote the name of the man they wanted to be exiled on a broken pot sherd (or *ostrakon*, hence the name "ostracism"). The man with the greatest number of votes was ostracized. Ostracism was first used in 487 B.C.E., and the last recorded case was around 416 B.C.E.

These pot sherds were found in excavations in the Athenian agora (or marketplace). They were used to vote on which politician ought to be sent into exile.

During the mid-fifth century B.C.E., large sums of money were spent on a great building program at Athens. Many of the buildings on the Athenian acropolis were built to replace temples destroyed by the Persians during the Persian Wars (490–479 B.C.E.)

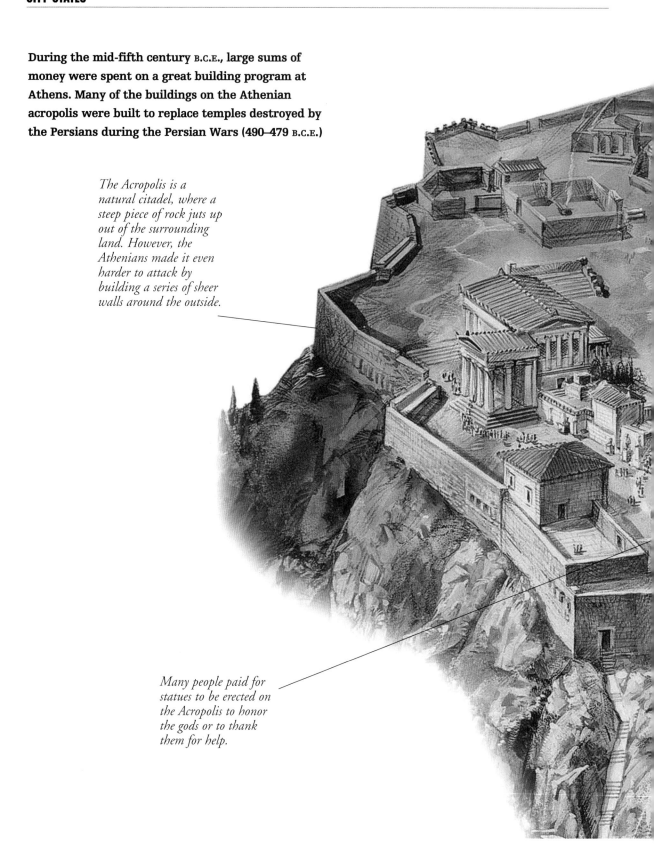

The Acropolis is a natural citadel, where a steep piece of rock juts up out of the surrounding land. However, the Athenians made it even harder to attack by building a series of sheer walls around the outside.

Many people paid for statues to be erected on the Acropolis to honor the gods or to thank them for help.

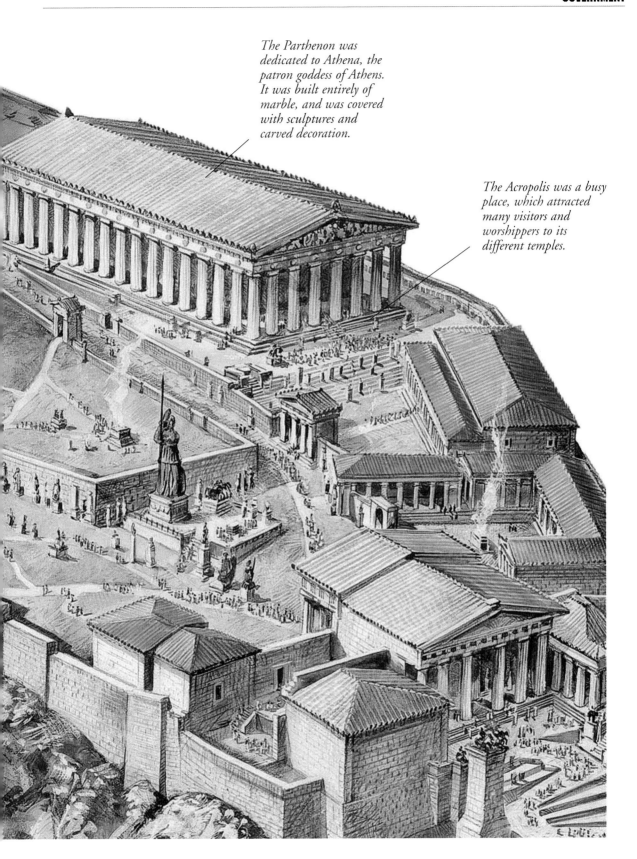

The Parthenon was dedicated to Athena, the patron goddess of Athens. It was built entirely of marble, and was covered with sculptures and carved decoration.

The Acropolis was a busy place, which attracted many visitors and worshippers to its different temples.

Chapter Two

Trade and Commerce

One of the main occupations in ancient Greece was farming, even though much of Greece is mountainous and difficult to cultivate. Grain crops (such as wheat or barley) were grown in coastal regions, where there was fertile soil and a good rainfall. However, the soil in most parts of Greece was not capable of producing large quantities of arable crops. Instead, farmers often produced other goods. Vines were cultivated for grapes on hillier ground. Some grapes would be eaten as fruit, but most grapes would be used to make wine. Olive trees were planted on the poorest soil. Olives were a very important part of the Greek economy. Not only were olives a tasty part of a meal, they were also used to make olive oil, which provided oil for heating and cooking, as well as being used as a kind of soap.

Greek farms were not large. They produced enough food to feed the farmer and his family and to provide a small surplus to be sold at the market. Rich men might own a lot of land, but usually this land would be managed as several smaller farms, rather than one large estate.

It was rare to have enough land to pasture large animals, such as cows or horses. One part of Greece, called Thessaly, had so much rich land compared to the rest of Greece that it was known as "horse-breeding Thessaly." Elsewhere only the rich could afford to keep horses. Other animals were more common on Greek farms. Plowing was done by oxen and mules, and donkeys were used to carry goods to and from market. Goats

This sixth-century B.C.E. black figure vase shows farmers collecting the olive harvest. A large number of Greeks worked on the land.

The agricultural land near Athens was not good for growing arable crops, so many Athenian farmers cultivated olive trees. Athenian olive oil was traded throughout the Mediterranean region.

and sheep grazed on hillsides. Not only did they provide meat and milk, but also their coats were a source of wool, and their skins could be cured to make leather. Hens and chickens were kept to provide eggs and meat. Farmers might also keep bees to provide the honey that was used to sweeten food.

The Marketplace

A family could not meet all its needs from its own land. Trade was essential and there would be a marketplace, or *agora* (*AGG-oh-rah*), in every town. The agora was a very important place, not just for trade, but also for social meetings, since friends would meet each other and talk while they were out shopping.

A vast range of activities went on in the agora. In one corner, there were farmers selling vegetables, cheese, eggs, and fruit. Nearby there were olive oil sellers, fish sellers, and old women selling garlands or flowers. There might be a stall offering drinks and cooked snacks. Barbers would cut hair and trim beards. Other stalls offered finished products, such as shoes, books, armor, knives, vases, and textiles. Bankers, moneylenders, and money changers (who exchanged the various coins used in the different city-states for coins used in their own city-state) would be

Fishing and Island Life

Fish was a very important part of the Greek diet. Beef was expensive and rarely eaten, but many Greek towns and villages had easy access to the sea. Fish was cheap and provided a good alternative to meat, and fishermen caught many types of fish. Octopus was considered a great delicacy. Being a fisherman was a common occupation, but there were also others who worked at sea, such as sailors, and sponge-divers, who brought up sponges from the sea bed and sold them for use in the home.

Fish was an important part of the ancient Greeks' diet. This wall painting from the fifteenth century B.C.E. shows a fisherman with his catch.

carrying out their business. There were even philosophers discussing politics, and promising to teach men how to think. In another area, men looking for work would gather together and offer their skills as cooks, entertainers, acrobats, or general laborers. Slaves would also be displayed for sale, while the slave dealer listed what they were trained to do. There were also workshops near the agora where bronze workers, jewelers, sculptors, lyre makers, rope makers, and potters were all at work. Everywhere there would be a great deal of noise and activity, and visiting the agora was an excellent method of keeping up to date with news and gossip about the great figures of the city.

Imports and Exports

Not every Greek city-state could produce all the materials and goods that its population wanted to buy. For example, Athens was a great producer of olive oil and painted pottery, but could not grow all the grain she required to feed her population. Athens had to import a great deal of grain from the Black Sea region.

The harbors were very busy places where you could find everything from wine, olive oil, honey, grain, dates, cheese, pigs, and horses to spices, gold, wool, ivory, and rugs. Some of the items had traveled over a great distance. Timber, which was essential for building ships, was imported from the north of Greece; papyrus, used to make books, came from Egypt, and silk for fine clothes came from China. Other imports were small, but very expensive items, such as gems or murex, a purple dye made from sea snails and used to

Tax

With so much trade taking place, customs charges were often made on imports. Such charges raised useful revenue for the state, although they did make the products more expensive. The state of Sparta, however, did not approve of luxury goods or of Spartan citizens hoarding money and taking part in trade. Coins were not introduced into Sparta until the fourth century B.C.E. Until then, Spartans had used barter (exchanging one product for another) or iron bars, which were an early form of currency.

dye clothes a fashionable color. Raw materials, such as copper, silver, and flax for making linen cloth, were traded, as well as finished products, including statues, pots, books, and metalwork.

Trade and Travel

Most of Greece is close to the sea, and communication was usually much easier by sea than by land. It was certainly less difficult to transport goods by sea, rather than hauling them by pack-mule over steep, mountainous terrain. Moreover, travel by land was not always safe, as robbers and bandits lay in wait to attack travelers in lonely places.

While merchants who sailed across the seas buying and selling goods could make large profits, trade was a risky business. Most ships were small, and had a single mast with a large rectangular sail. Navigation was difficult and there was always the danger of sudden storms. Little traveling was done during the winter months, when the seas were rough. Even in summer, ships tended to keep close to the land so that they could race for harbor if a storm blew up. However, the large numbers of Greek shipwrecks that have been discovered by underwater archaeologists demonstrate that many ships were lost despite these precautions. Another

This black figure vase dates from the mid-sixth century B.C.E. and shows the god Dionysus sailing in a typical small Greek vessel.

Meals and Dinner Parties

The Greeks started the day with a light breakfast of fruit or bread dipped in olive oil or wine. Lunch was also fairly light, consisting of bread accompanied by olives, cheese, or figs. Supper tended to be made up of soup, fish, or eggs. However, dinner party menus were much more extensive and consisted of several courses.

Dinner parties might start off with nibbles which were designed to stimulate the appetite, such as olives, radishes, or onions. The main course might consist of fish, eels, or poultry (such as quails or other birds). This main dish was served with a sauce or some side dishes, such as vegetables. To follow, there could be a selection of salted almonds, dried figs, nuts, grapes, or other fruit, and perhaps some sweet pastries. This was all washed down with sweet wine, diluted with water. At this point the discussion, or symposium (*sim-POE-zee-um*) started. Here the guests would drink wine together and talk about politics and philosophy, or play the lyre and sing. Guests wore garlands and were sprinkled with perfume. Greeks normally ate with their fingers, so throughout the meal there was water to wash hands. Dinner parties were strictly for men and it would have been considered shocking for the host's female relatives to attend.

Men enjoyed relaxing at dinner parties. They did not sit at tables, but reclined on couches and ate their food with their fingers. Wine was drunk from specially shaped drinking cups.

danger when sailing was the presence of pirates, who made a living by raiding merchant ships. They seized the cargoes of the ships, but sometimes also captured the crew and any passengers and sold them to slave traders as slaves.

Chapter Three

Pastimes and Ceremonies

While the ancient Greeks enjoyed a variety of sports, including hunting and chariot racing, their main sporting activity was athletics, which they took very seriously. Although Greek boys began athletics when they were young, they continued to exercise regularly even when they were much older. Greek men liked to stay healthy and it was a matter of pride to be a good athlete. Moreover, city-states saw athletic training as a method of keeping men in good shape physically for when they might be needed to fight in a war. There were many special exercise grounds throughout Greece and many athletic competitions, both at local and inter-state levels. Top athletes came from across Greece to compete in the four great inter-state games held at Corinth, Nemea, Delphi, and Olympia.

The Olympic Games

The Olympic Games were held in honor of Zeus, the ruler of the gods, every four years at Olympia. They were first held in 776 B.C.E. and ended in the late fourth century C.E. The games were considered so important by the Greeks that a special sacred truce was called between warring states for a month before and after the games, to enable competitors and spectators to travel to Olympia without danger. Once the truce had been called and the competitors, trainers, judges, supporters, and spectators had arrived, the festival started. It consisted of a mixture of religious activity and athletic events, and lasted for five days.

Sport and athletics were important to the Greeks and they greatly enjoyed local and inter-state competitions. Much Greek art reflected this interest in competitions. This red figure vase painting shows a discus thrower twisting around ready to hurl his discus.

This marble relief shows an unusual sport played with sticks and a ball which seems to resemble field hockey.

There was a variety of events at the Olympic Games and they were held at different places. Boxing and wrestling took place in a small sandy arena, chariot races and horse races took place at a special racetrack, and running events took place in the Stadium. The Stadium was around 600 feet (182 meters) long and had room for over 20,000 spectators. Races consisted of three lengths: 200 yards (182 meters), 400 yards (366 meters), and nearly three miles (4.8 kilometers). Most events were run naked, but there was a special race with competitors wearing armor and carrying a shield. This event was physically very demanding and reflected the importance of keeping fit for war.

Some of the competitions at the Olympic Games were very violent. Boxers wound

Boys and Girls

Boys between the ages of twelve and eighteen were allowed to compete at special events in the Olympic Games. These events were boxing, wrestling, and running. Events were split into age categories, and successful boy competitors would return to compete in the adult Olympic Games when they were older. Girls and women were treated rather differently. They were banned from Olympia on pain of death during the time of the Olympic Games. However, they were allowed to take part in a separate festival, called the Heraia (*HEH-riy-ah*), held in honor of Hera (who was married to Zeus). This festival was also held every four years and featured three running events for the girls.

Wrestling was a dangerous sport. This Greek vase shows two judges or trainers watching the wrestlers to see that no cheating took place.

leather straps around their hands to give their blows extra force. Such leather straps could easily cut into skin, and boxers often had unpleasant cuts and bruises. Moreover, boxers were allowed to punch their opponent anywhere on his body. The contest ended when an athlete gave up or was knocked unconscious. This meant that fighting could last for over an hour!

Wrestling was even more violent, particularly one event called the *pankration* (*pan-KRAH-tee-on*). The pankration had only two rules. Competitors were not allowed to bite their opponent or gouge out his eyes. Everything else was legal. This meant that wrestlers could attempt to strangle each other, knee opponents in the stomach, and deliberately break their fingers. Not surprisingly, some competitors died in these events.

Winning a Wreath

Top athletes competing in the inter-state Panhellenic (or all-Greek) Games did not win large sums of money. Instead, they were presented with a wreath made of leaves. Winners at the Olympic Games were presented with an olive wreath, victors at the Pythian (*PITH-ee-un*) Games (held at Delphi) won a laurel wreath, and those who triumphed at the Isthmian (*ISTH-mee-an*) Games (at Corinth) and the Nemean Games (at Nemea, near Argos) were crowned with wreaths of wild celery.

Cheating

Cheating seems to have been relatively rare at the Olympic Games. There are some stories of people being bribed to lose events, but these are not common. Any cheating resulted in a beating or a fine. Fines were devoted to Zeus, and those who broke the rules might be ordered to pay for a statue to be erected at the entrance to the sanctuary at Olympia. Such statues served to remind competitors of the importance of keeping to the rules.

Wrestling was also included in the pentathlon, which was a mixed competition consisting of five different events. These were running, jumping, wrestling, javelin throwing, and discus throwing. Special aids were used in the jumping and javelin-throwing events. Athletes employed heavy jumping weights to help to propel themselves forward, and a twist of leather was used when throwing the javelin. This helped the javelin to stay on course and may have sent it forward further than throwing it by hand.

Equestrian events were exciting because they were dangerous. Chariot racing consisted of two- or four-horse chariots racing twelve laps around the racetrack. Collisions were common, particularly when as many as forty chariots might be taking part. Crashes most often occurred when chariots tried to turn around the bends at either end of the track. Here the horses were turning in a narrow semi-circle and not all maintained their footing. Horse races were held over the same course and were equally exciting. Jockeys rode without stirrups, and were often thrown from their mounts.

Medicine and Illness

The Greeks recognized the importance of keeping fit, and their festival games helped to encourage men to exercise and keep healthy. However, despite this emphasis on health, ancient Greeks tended to die earlier

A Rich Man's Game

Chariot racing was an activity of the rich. Horses were expensive to keep and only a rich man could afford to devote the time and expense necessary to train a team of chariot horses. However, these rich men rarely drove in the races. Instead, they often paid a professional chariot driver to race the horses. If he won, the glory and credit for the victory went to the owner, not the driver.

One story survives that shows how costly and impressive chariot racing was. During the Peloponnesian War (431–404 B.C.E.), Athens had reached the point where other states believed that she was exhausted and without resources. A rich man called Alcibiades (*Al-see-BYE-uh-deez*) entered not just one chariot in the Olympic Games, but seven! His chariots came first, second, and fourth, and he argued that this showed other Greeks that Athenians still had enough wealth to take part in a sport restricted to rich men. So impressive was the victory that the other Greeks came to believe that Athens was in a better position financially than she really was.

Doctors faced a wide variety of diseases without any modern medical aids. This doctor is "bleeding" his patient. The Greeks believed that extracting a certain amount of blood might help to cure fevers and other illnesses.

than people in the Western world today. Most adults died in their forties and fifties and many children never reached their teens. Also, many men were killed in war and women often died in childbirth. Although the ancient Greeks thought carefully about medicine and how to cure ill people, there were no antibiotics, anesthetics, or modern medical aids, such as X-rays or scanners. Death rates from contagious (easily spread) illnesses could be very high, as was shown in 430 to 427 B.C.E., when plague struck Athens and about one-third of the population died.

Sacred Snakes!

In Greek mythology, Asclepius was the son of the god Apollo, who was also concerned with medicine. In statues or pictures, Asclepius is usually shown leaning on a staff. Wrapped around this staff is a snake. The snake was a particularly appropriate symbol for Asclepius because the Greeks believed that a snake could refresh and renew itself when it shed its skin.

Asclepius' medical aid was also supposed to help human beings to be revived. Owing to the connection with snakes, all the sanctuaries of Asclepius had pits where sacred snakes were kept. Sometimes these snakes were credited with healing patients—there are stories of a snake licking a patient's toe and his foot disease being cured!

This stone carving shows a doctor examining a patient. Asclepius, the god of medicine, watches on the right-hand side. He can be recognized by the snake twisting around his staff.

Asclepius (*Ah-SKLEE-pee-uss*) was the god of healing and had an important role in Greek medicine. Sick people visited shrines of Asclepius where they carried out sacrifices to the god. Then priests gave them medicine and some advice as to how to look after themselves. However, the most important act was to sleep overnight in the Temple of Asclepius. Either the god would heal them while they slept, or he might speak to them in a dream and tell them what treatment would cure them. The greatest of the shrines to Asclepius was the large complex at Epidauros. As well as the Temple to Asclepius, it contained accommodations, baths, and a huge theater where people could watch plays.

The Hippocratic Oath

Hippocrates and his followers were not just concerned with treating people, they were also concerned about medical ethics and how doctors ought to behave. The Hippocratic Oath was drawn up to give doctors some guidelines as to how to act and it is still sworn by many doctors today. Under the Hippocratic Oath, doctors swear that they will help the sick to the best of their ability, that they will not do any harm, and that they will never attempt to take advantage of their position, for example, by telling people confidential information about a patient.

Greek medicine made advances under Hippocrates (around 460–380 B.C.E.) and his followers. Hippocrates believed that it was important to discover the causes of an illness and to treat the causes with the appropriate medicine. Patients were examined and symptoms were noted. Herbal medicines or special diets were often prescribed and good doctors noted how the medicine affected the patient. Careful, rational observation enabled doctors to assess whether the medicine normally helped patients and was a good medicine to prescribe. Even though methods of treating disease have greatly changed with the arrival of new drugs, Hippocrates' scientific approach to illness still underlies much of modern medicine and medical research.

Death and Funerals

When even the best Greek medicine could not save a patient, it was necessary to prepare the body for burial. The ancient Greeks believed that it was essential to carry out the

The Greeks believed that when someone died they were rowed across the Styx River to the Underworld by Charon, the ferryman of the dead.

The most important shrine to the god Asclepius was at Epidauros. Large numbers of people visited the sanctuary each year in the hope of finding a cure for their illness.

This building, known as the Tholos, was very unusual. Most Greek buildings are rectangular, but this temple is circular.

Patients slept in this building, hoping that Asclepius would visit them while they slept and cure them.

This temple was dedicated to Asclepius and was built in 380 B.C.E. to replace an older temple.

Many statues and smaller offerings were dedicated by grateful patients who believed that Asclepius had cured them.

The size and splendor of the buildings at Epidauros reflected how many people visited the site and dedicated offerings to the god.

This image from a Greek vase shows a Greek funeral procession. The mourners are dressed in dark clothes and the women cover their heads in grief.

correct ritual when dealing with dead bodies. If bodies were not properly buried, the soul would spend eternity wandering around looking for a home.

First the body was bathed and anointed with oil. Then it was dressed in linen, a wreath was placed on its head, and it was laid out on a bier (or special table) to be displayed to mourners. Finally, a small coin known as an *obol* was placed in the dead person's mouth, so that he or she would be able to pay Charon, the man who ferried the souls of the dead across the Styx River to the Underworld. Relatives sang songs expressing their grief and prayed to Hermes, the messenger god. Hermes was believed to accompany dead souls into the Underworld and mourners begged him to look after the dead person as he or she traveled down to the Underworld.

The Underworld

The Underworld was ruled over by Hades (also known as Pluto). The entry to the Underworld was guarded by the fierce three-headed dog, Cerberus, who prevented anyone from escaping. Once a soul had paid Charon a fee and had been rowed across the river Styx, it was brought before three judges to be judged on how it had lived its life. These judges sent the very good to the Elysian Fields, where they lived a happy life of pleasure in the sunlight. Most people were sent to the Asphodel Fields. Here there was no sunlight or fun. Souls wandered around in the gloom, waiting for offerings to be sent to them by relatives. Those who had been very wicked on Earth were sent to Tartarus. Tartarus was a place of eternal damnation, where people suffered constant torment as punishment for their evil ways.

After a day of mourning, the body was taken to a cemetery in a cart. A procession of relatives followed the cart and watched the burial. Rich people would hire professional mourners to accompany the cart and to demonstrate the importance of the dead person by increasing the size of a funeral procession. Women mourners cried out, beat their breasts, and tore at their hair and faces. They might also cut off a lock of hair and give it to the dead person.

At the cemetery the body was either cremated or buried. If it was cremated, the ashes were placed in a special funeral vase and this was then buried in the tomb. If the body was buried, it was either placed directly in the tomb (perhaps in a wooden coffin) or was placed in a stone coffin, known as a sarcophagus. Often special vessels decorated with scenes of mourning were filled with food and drink, and placed alongside the body for use in the afterlife. A raised stone slab, known as a *stele* (*STEH-leh*), might be erected above the grave. Such slabs often showed a representation of the dead person and reflected the grief felt by relatives at their loss. Women brought offerings to the tomb for many days after the funeral. Offerings would also be made on the birthday of the dead person and on the anniversary of their death.

Chapter Four

Childhood and Education

Greek children of both sexes were generally loved by their parents, but boys and girls lived very different lives. Girls were educated at home by their mothers and learned how to run a household. They may have learned to read and write, but they were not normally taught to appreciate literature or to think about politics. Boys, on the other hand, studied a much wider range of subjects, including reading, writing, geography, music, and athletics. Greek education for boys was designed to produce good citizens who respected the state, obeyed its laws, and could defend it when necessary.

Babies and Infants

Greek babies were born at home. The mother would have a midwife to help her during the birth, and the other women of the household would probably also be present. Childbirth could be a dangerous business and many women and babies died from infection after the birth. To help prevent infection, the newborn baby was washed in water (or wine, at Sparta) before it was wrapped up in swaddling clothes (long bands of cloth). The child would be shown to the father, and it was up to him to decide whether it would be reared or not. If he did not want to bring up the child (perhaps

This tombstone shows a woman with a small child. Many women died in childbirth and a considerable number of children would have lost their mother at a young age.

because he could not afford to, or because the child was disabled), he would refuse to acknowledge it. This meant that the child would be abandoned and left outside to die. Because boys were valued more highly than girls, baby girls were more likely to be exposed than boys. Occasionally, a passerby would rescue such abandoned babies, but if this happened they would normally be brought up as slaves.

If the baby did not die shortly after birth, and the father acknowledged it, the next stage in a baby's life came when it was five days old. At this stage, it was formally introduced to the rest of the family, brought to the hearth of the house, and presented to the household gods. This was a time of rejoicing, and a party was held to celebrate the arrival of the new member of the household. On the tenth day after birth, another party was held to commemorate the naming of the baby. Boys were often named after their grandfather and the "name-day" was celebrated every year, just as we celebrate birthdays. The next major milestone in a child's life was when he or she reached the age of three. At this stage, children were believed to have left infancy behind and received a small jug to mark this important step.

Not many toys have survived from ancient Greece, partly because the materials from which they were made have easily rotted over time. Babies were given clay rattles shaped like animals and little children played with clay dolls, dressed in fabric cloaks. Toy chariots and horses have also been found, and may have been the source of exciting make-believe races. Children also had hoops, tops, and kites to play with. Some kept birds, dogs, or tortoises as pets. As today, children also enjoyed playing games with each other. Boys enjoyed pretending to be soldiers or generals directing battles. Girls may well have played at keeping house.

Small children were brought up at home, often by their mother. When a boy was around the age of seven, he would attend school and would move out of the feminine surroundings of home into the masculine world of the city-state.

Basic Education

Most existing evidence for education comes from Athens, so it is not certain that most Greek states followed a similar system. It is clear that education was

When children reached the age of three, they were presented with a special wine jug to mark their emergence from babyhood. Such wine jugs were often decorated with scenes from childhood, such as this picture of a boy playing on a hobby-horse.

regarded as important in Athens, and it seems that most boys attended school. Education was not provided by the state, but paid for by parents. Athenian boys started school around the age of seven, and would attend three teachers—a *grammatistes* (*gram-ah-TEES-tehz*), who taught him to read and write (the Greek word for a letter is *gramma*); a *kitharistes* (*kith-ah-REES-tehz*), who taught him to play a musical instrument; and a *paidotribes* (*pai-doh-TREE-behz*), who gave him athletic training. These teachers did not work together in a single school, but ran their own establishments, and boys would have to travel between the three separate school buildings during the school day.

Reading and Writing

The main task of the grammatistes was to teach boys to read and write. However, they also taught basic arithmetic, and some offered geometry, geography, and drawing. Children used wax tablets, on which they wrote with a double-ended metal pen. The sharp end was used to scratch letters, and the blunt end to smooth out mistakes. Wax tablets could be used again and again, and were cheap. When children grew more skillful at writing, they began to write on paper made from papyrus reeds. Ink was made from soot, or the natural ink found in cuttlefish and squid.

Once the basic letters had been mastered, boys were introduced to selections from the great poets. Poetry was chosen not just for its quality of language, but also to teach good values, such as courage or honor. The poems of Homer were particularly popular, and boys learned long passages by heart.

Boys were often escorted to and from school by a slave called a *paidogogus* (*PAID-oh-go-guss*), or "boy-leader." This slave carried the boy's books and musical instruments, but he was also equipped with a cane and would beat the boy if he misbehaved during lessons or in the street. Corporal punishment was normal in schools, and teachers would beat boys who did not work hard enough or pay proper attention in class.

Schools were small and often consisted of a single room, equipped with stools or benches.

Laws on Education

Education in Athens was very much in the hands of parents, who chose which schools their sons would attend. However, the Athenian state had some influence on education. It paid for the education of certain boys, whose fathers had been killed fighting for Athens and it also provided *gymnasia*, or training-grounds, which were open to all at no cost. No attempt was made to lay down what was to be studied and there seems to have been little legislation on matters such as class sizes, school holidays, or school buildings. Ancient sources record that parents had to ensure that children made the journey to and from school in daylight, but otherwise there seems to have been little state regulation of education. Matters concerning education were handled very differently in Sparta, where the entire curriculum was laid down by the state.

The Difficulties of Reading

In classical times, punctuation was not used. There were no commas to split up sections of the sentence, and no periods to mark the ends of sentences. However, the greatest obstacle to reading fluently was that there were no spaces between individual words. This made it difficult to see where each word started and finished (imaginereadingasentencewhichiswrittenlikethis!)

The ancient Greeks did not read in silence, but muttered the words to themselves as they read. All this must have made the task of learning to read challenging, but most Athenians were sufficiently literate to be able to read notices in the agora, or marketplace. Many more were capable of reading complex texts, which demanded a wide vocabulary and the ability to follow difficult arguments.

Greek laws and other records were engraved on stone for all to read. However, the task of reading such documents was made harder because they were written in capital letters, often without spaces between the words.

There were no desks. Some classes were even held in courtyards in the open air, although the noise of passersby must have been a distraction! There were no long school holidays, but schools closed when festivals were celebrated. There were many festivals held around February, and this time must have been popular with pupils and schoolmasters alike.

Although it was considered important to be educated, schoolmasters were not highly rated. School fees were low and teaching was not a well-paid profession. Moreover, many parents did not respect their sons' teachers, particularly as some of the assistant teachers were slaves.

Music

Music was a very important part of life in ancient Greece. It was played at private occasions, such as banquets, and public occasions, such as festivals. People were married to the sound of singing, and the dead were laid to rest accompanied by music. There were competitions for singers and instrumentalists at the various Greek games, and they attracted entries from the finest musicians. Winners of these events received the same level of honor as athletes. In Athens, it was considered normal for a man to be able to entertain his guests by singing to them, or playing the lyre. Moreover, plays performed at the dramatic festivals featured choruses sung by citizens. Music was therefore a key part of an Athenian boy's education.

Unfortunately, it is not really known what ancient Greek music sounded like. It certainly did not follow the conventions of Western classical music, which is based on tones and semi-tones. It probably sounded rather like Arabic or Indian music. However, it is known that most music was for the voice, or string and wind instruments.

The Greeks sang many different types of song. Some were sung at home, some on stage, and some when marching into battle. Poetry was also set to music. Here, careful attention was paid to ensure that the style of the music was appropriate to the words of the poem. Music was also used to make things easier to learn by heart—for example, the laws of Athens were set to music for children to memorize. Songs were accompanied by string or wind instruments, but such instruments could also be played on their own. The main string instrument was the lyre, which had seven strings, and was rather like a guitar. It

Music was an essential part of every Greek boy's education. This young man is playing the lyre.

Other Instruments and Musical Terms

The lyre, kithara, and aulos were the most common ancient Greek musical instruments. However, there were others. The *sambuca* (*sam-BOOK-ah*) was a type of harp. The *syrinx* (*sirr-inks*) was similar to a set of pan pipes. There was a trumpet called the *salpinx* (*SAL-pinks*) and a curved horn, known as a *keras* (*KEH-rass*). Percussion instruments were also used, although they were not considered to be suitable for serious music. These included tambourines, or *tympana* (*TOOM-pana*), cymbals, or *kymbala*, (*KOOM-bala*), and castanets, known as *crotala* (*KROW-tala*). Many modern musical terms are derived directly from Greek. These include "harmony," "chord," "melody," "rhythm," "tone," and "music" itself. Other Greek words are also in use today, although their meanings have changed somewhat. Three such words are *orchestra, symphony,* and *tympana.* The orchestra was originally a place where the chorus of a play danced. It now means a large group of instrumentalists playing together. Symphony originally meant music, but it is now used to mean a piece of music for a large number of instruments. Tympana was the Greek word for tambourines. The spelling has changed into *tympani,* which are the large drums played in an orchestra.

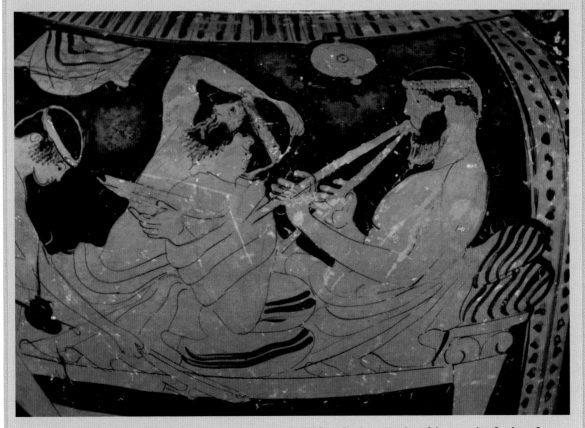

Men often entertained their guests at dinner parties by playing music. This man is playing the aulos, or double flute.

consisted of a sound box to amplify (make louder) the sound. This sound box was made of leather stretched over the shell of a tortoise. Two thin curved sidepieces made from wood or horn came up from the sound box, and were connected at the top with a thin crosspiece. The strings were stretched from the crosspiece down to the tortoise shell. The strings could then be plucked to produce a sound, which would resonate through the sound box. A slightly larger version of the lyre, known as a *kithara* (*KITH-ah-rah*), was made of wood. The main wind instrument was the *aulos* (*AW-loss*). This was a double flute, although it was held and sounded much more like a modern oboe than a modern flute.

As well as athletics, Greek children also enjoyed other games, such as playing with a hoop.

Learning To Be an Athlete

Outdoor education and physical training were valued highly by the ancient Greeks, who wanted their sons to grow up to be fit and healthy. Boys who were fit were also better suited to the rigors of military service, and politicians believed that it was important to encourage exercise to enable men to fight more effectively for the state. Gymnastics was an essential part of this physical training.

Gymnastics was taught in separate schools, known as *palaestra* (*pah-LAI-strah*). These schools were equipped with sandy floors where exercises were carried out. Boys were grouped according to age and ability. The aim was to build up a strong body, and the needs of each boy were carefully considered by his trainer, who devised programs of exercises to strengthen his muscles without putting him

The Gymnasium

Today a gymnasium is an indoor sports hall. However, the first gymnasia were large public sports grounds in the open air. These complexes contained a variety of exercise areas, such as a running track, a jumping ground, a palaestra for exercising, and a parade ground. Athens had three large gymnasia, which were funded by the state. They were open to boys and men and there was no entrance charge, as Athenians wanted their citizens to keep fit and healthy. One of the three gymnasia was called the Academy, and was situated outside Athens next to a river. Here Athenians might also hear visiting teachers give lectures—the Academy was a place where both the mind and the body were to be stretched and exercised.

Boys were taught to read and write at school. This boy is using a double-ended metal pen to scratch the wax surface of the tablet. Children were also taught to play musical instruments, such as the lyre, which is hanging up on the wall.

Education for Girls

Girls were not thought to be able to carry out the "masculine" tasks of running the state or making laws and voting on political matters. Therefore, they received a very different education from boys. Some girls, particularly in richer households, were taught to read by their mothers. However, the main purpose of girls' education was to train them to be good wives and mothers. This meant that they learned how to run a house and bring up a family. Much of this would have been taught by example. Girls would watch their mothers, help them to do the housework, and look after children. Girls would also be taught how to spin wool, weave cloth, sew, and cook. Daughters of a rich household would also learn how to supervise slaves, and ensure that the family finances were properly managed.

Although much of a girl's time was spent carrying out household tasks, there was also time for other activities, such as performing special dances at religious ceremonies. This pot painting shows a girl learning a dance.

under too much strain. Many exercises were performed to music to help with the timing of the moves, and boys practiced naked so that their trainers could see how their bodies and muscles responded to the exercises.

Of course, this physical education did not just consist of exercises. The boys also learned to run and jump, to throw the javelin and the discus, to box, and to wrestle. There would have been rivalry between the children as they tried to beat each other in the various events and the best might be put forward to compete in inter-state competitions.

Public Speaking

Children from poorer families probably left school around the age of twelve or fourteen, because their parents needed them to earn money. They would start work, either in the family business or farm, or as apprentices. The children of wealthy families would continue being educated until the age of eighteen, when they were required to undertake two years of military service.

Education for older boys was intended to teach them to take a full part in running the state. One of the key skills for a politician in ancient Athens was the ability to speak well in public and, at fourteen, a boy would start to learn how to compose a good speech and deliver it to an audience. Rhetoric (*RET-or-ik*), or the art of public speaking, was learned from specialist teachers, known as *rhetors* (*RAY-tors*). A boy would study famous speeches by great generals and politicians. He would also hear his relatives discussing politics, and learn from their example. As well as rhetoric, boys could also undertake further study in mathematics, philosophy, and astronomy.

Military Service

At the age of eighteen, all Athenian citizens had to undergo two years of military service. This meant that Athens had a reserve of trained men on whom she could call to serve in the army during a war. Young men doing their military training were known as *ephebes* (*EFF-eebz*) and were paid a small amount of money to buy their food. The first year was spent living in barracks and learning how to use various weapons. The second year was passed serving in the various forts situated along the Athenian borders. Ephebes who served in cavalry units had to provide their own horses. Such units would have been staffed by youths from rich families. Ephebes had to swear an oath that they would not disgrace their weapons or desert their comrades. They also swore to leave their homeland greater and better than they found it, and to obey the laws and honor the temples.

Part of the importance of military training was to learn to march in formation. This seventh-century B.C.E. vase also shows an aulos-player, piping the soldiers into battle.

Growing Up in Sparta

Life in Sparta was very different from life in other Greek states. Sparta was a military society whose citizens were expected to devote their lives to serving the state. Girls were trained for motherhood and boys' education was based on military principles, suitable for would-be soldiers. Above all, the emphasis was on strict discipline and high levels of physical fitness.

Spartan women were very fit and took part in lots of exercise. Women who were pregnant exercised daily to ensure that they gave birth to a strong, healthy baby. When the child was born, its father presented it to a group of old men from his tribe. These men inspected the child. If it was healthy, the father was allowed to take it home and rear it, but if it was weak or seemed ill, it was exposed on a mountainside and left to die.

Children were brought up by their mothers until they were seven, but mothers were not encouraged to spoil their children. Young Spartans were expected to eat plain food without complaining. They had to get used to the dark and being left on their own, and they were not expected to be bad tempered or to cry. At the age of seven, boys started their main education. They left their mothers and joined a group of sixty other boys. The boy who showed the best judgment and the strongest fighting spirit would be made the leader. Other boys had to obey his instructions. There were also older boys who acted as prefects and urged the younger boys to be competitive and brave at all times.

Boys learned to read and write and to do some basic arithmetic. Music was highly valued and both boys and girls sang in competitions. Sparta also had a reputation for producing good performers, both on the lyre and aulos. Apart from this, there was little intellectual training. Instead, the emphasis was on rigorous physical pursuits to make Spartans tough, obedient, and determined. Wrestling, running, discus and javelin throwing, and drill to music were all practiced. Boys were also encouraged to fight each other and not to show fear. Discipline was very strict. Disobedience or slowness to carry out routine orders was punished with beatings and boys who cried out in pain were despised by their friends.

As boys grew older, their physical training intensified. Once they were twelve they were

Spartan Girls

Girls' education included music and dancing, but the main emphasis was on gymnastic training to make them fit and strong, so that they could bear robust children. Unlike other Greek girls, Spartan girls did not spend time learning to weave and spin. They were not expected to perform occupations that required them to sit down. Instead, girls ran, wrestled, and threw the discus and javelin. They took part in athletic competitions, and other Greeks noted in horror that Spartan girls exercised naked.

given only one cloak a year, and they were not allowed to wear a tunic or underclothes. Their hair was cut short and they went barefoot, whatever the weather. They slept on beds made of rushes gathered from the river, and washed by swimming in cold water. They were only allowed to have baths and oil their bodies a few days each year. All of this training was meant to make them used to bearing the harsh conditions a soldier might have to endure.

Spartan youths were also trained to live off the land. Boys were given only meager rations. If they wanted more food they had to steal it. If they were caught, they were whipped, not

because it was wrong to steal, but because they had been caught, and had not achieved their aim. Young Spartans also had to obey the orders of their prefects, as well as their instructors, without any argument. The prefects punished them with whippings if they disobeyed. At eighteen or nineteen, boys became full soldiers, and at twenty-four, they were front-line soldiers. At the age of thirty, a Spartan became a full citizen and was allowed to set up his own house with a wife and family. However, any boy who did not manage to pass through his training would not be allowed to become a full Spartan citizen. Failure to do so would bring great dishonor to him and his family, and most boys would do everything they could not to suffer such a disgrace.

The Spartans believed that it was vital that young boys were forced to undergo rigorous military training. Only then would they be capable of putting their country before themselves, as had King Leonidas and the 300 Spartans who died at the Battle of Thermopylae in 480 B.C.E.

The Fox and the Boy

Spartans considered it very important to be able to bear pain without flinching. One famous story recorded the case of a Spartan boy who had stolen a fox cub and hidden it inside his cloak. Rather than be caught carrying the animal, he let it bite and claw his stomach so badly that he died. The Spartans also held a competition where boys tried to snatch as many cheeses from an altar as possible. To get near the altar, they had to run past men holding whips. It was impossible to seize the cheese without being badly beaten, but the boy who grabbed the most cheeses won the competition. In Roman times there was another competition where boys were whipped at an altar. The boy who was whipped the most without crying out was honored the most. However, some boys died during these savage beatings.

Chapter Five

Women and Domestic Life

Ancient Greek domestic life was very different from modern life in many ways. Ancient Greeks did not have the benefit of electricity, running water, or an efficient system of sewers. There were no labor-saving machines, and domestic tasks had to be carried out by hand. However, perhaps the greatest difference from today was the status of women. Most of our evidence for women's lives comes from ancient Athens, but it is clear that, in general, Greek women lacked the freedom that modern women enjoy socially, legally, economically, and politically.

Women were assumed to be vulnerable and in need of the guidance of men at all times. They were not allowed to live on their own, or with friends, but were forced to live with their nearest male relative. This relative acted as their guardian and legal representative and took care of any money (such as a marriage dowry) they possessed. Men believed that women lacked the ability to think rationally and, therefore, they were not given the vote and were unable to take part in politics. The role of women was very much restricted to the domestic sphere, where they were expected to run a household, bring up the children, and look after their husband. Athenian men believed that the greatest glory a woman could have was for men not to talk about her. Since very little writing by Greek women survives from the ancient world, it is not known whether they agreed with this assessment!

Women in ancient Greece worked hard running their homes and looking after their families, but they also enjoyed making themselves attractive. This Greek pot shows a woman checking her appearance in a mirror. The box in her left hand probably contained cosmetics or jewelry.

Women spent much of their time indoors, but some outdoor tasks, such as fetching water or picking fruit, gave them the chance to meet other women and talk to people outside their immediate family.

Marriage

Greek girls married young, usually between the ages of fourteen and eighteen. The marriage was arranged by the girl's father and the father of the man she was to marry. Greek men were often between thirty and thirty-five when they married for the first time, so a girl's husband was generally considerably older than she was. Some girls were married to men they had never met. Those who married male relatives might have had the opportunity to meet their future husbands at family occasions, such as funerals or other weddings, but would not have known him well. The selection of a

To Marry, or To Be Married

The Greek language reflects the different status of the bride and groom. When a Greek man announced that he was going to become a husband he would say, "I will marry this woman." However, a Greek girl had to use a different form of the verb "to marry." She was not allowed to have an active part in what was to happen—instead of also saying, "I will marry," she had to say, "I will be married to this man." This passive form of the verb reflected the passive role of the woman in marriage ceremonies.

Divorce

Divorce cases rarely came before the courts, and the ancient Greeks were able to end marriages without much difficulty. Most divorces were arranged by the husband. He renounced his wife by stating that he no longer wished to be married to her and sent her back to live with her family. Any children from the marriage would stay with their father. The most common cause for divorce was that the marriage had failed to produce any sons. In this case, the husband wanted to get rid of his existing wife in order to marry one who might bear him sons. If the woman's family suspected that a husband was wasting her dowry they could threaten him with divorce. On divorce, the dowry had to be repaid to the woman's family, and interest was added to the original sum.

husband lay with a girl's father, rather than with her. This lack of choice did not necessarily mean that a woman could not grow to love her husband, or be happy with him. However, marriage may often have been a frightening step into the unknown. A girl left her home and family to move into a new house with a husband she had hardly met, and a family she did not know. To make matters worse, she might now live some distance from her own family and childhood friends.

A girl's father paid a dowry, or a sum of money, to her husband. The size of the dowry would depend on the wealth of the girl's family. Naturally, a man wishing to marry a woman would consider how much money she would bring with her. Some ancient Greek authors preserve the complaints of poor men who lamented the fact that nobody would want to marry their daughters because they could not afford a dowry. A woman's husband controlled her dowry and could spend it as he pleased. In practice, however, most husbands would have been careful how they spent the money and would have invested it sensibly, in land or a small business.

After the marriage had been arranged, a ceremony took place to celebrate the engagement. The girl's father or guardian acknowledged the engagement, and a feast was often held. A large feast was also held on the day of the wedding. The night before the wedding, the bride had a special bath filled with sacred water drawn from holy springs. The water was brought using a particular kind of tall vase with long handles, called a *loutrophoros* (*LOO-tro-for-oss*). These vases were decorated with wedding scenes and were often buried in women's graves when they died.

The wedding was held at the house of the bride's father. Female relatives helped the bride to dress and to adjust the veil that hid her face. She then came forward to where the guests were waiting, wearing their best clothes and garlands of flowers. A fine feast was then held

Adoption in Athens

Some Athenians who did not have a son were so concerned about this that they adopted young men from other families. In return for taking on a new name and formally becoming part of their new family, these adopted sons would inherit the estate. The new father thus ensured that he would have a son to pay him honors once he was dead.

with much laughter, singing, and dancing. A special wedding cake, made with crushed sesame seeds and flour, was served at the feast, and the guests would throw sweets at the bride and groom.

When it grew dark, the newly married couple were taken to the groom's house in a chariot. Their friends and relatives followed, carrying wedding gifts to the girl's new home. Here, the bridegroom's mother would be waiting to welcome the bride inside the house. The

When the wedding ceremony was over and the feast was completed, a groom led his bride back to his new home, accompanied by friends and relatives.

bridegroom carried his wife over the threshold of the house and brought her to the hearth, which was the center of all Greek homes. Friends cried out in joy, and the couple were showered in dried fruit and nuts, which symbolized prosperity and the chance of having children. The husband then took his new wife to their bedroom and the guests sang a wedding song in their honor. At this point, the bride lifted her veil for the first time and all their guests departed.

Women's Activities in the Home

Men did not interest themselves with domestic tasks, so how well the household was managed and run depended on how good a manager his wife was. She oversaw all activities within the house, from cooking and cleaning to making the family's clothes. Women in richer families were also responsible for organizing any slaves they had, and ensuring that they carried out their duties properly. Women who lived in the country would probably also have helped on the farm, feeding the animals and collecting the eggs, as well as providing extra labor at harvest time.

The first duty of any wife, however, was to present her husband with a son. Daughters could not inherit the family estate and, if a man did not have a son, he had nobody who could carry on the direct family line and preserve his family name. There was enormous pressure on wives to have sons and there are tales from ancient Athens of women buying male babies so that they could pretend to their husbands that they had at last managed to give birth to a boy.

The Problems of Marriage

The Greek dramatist, Euripides (*You-RIP-ih-deez*), wrote a play about a woman called Medea (*Med-EE-ah*). Medea had been married to Jason and had helped him to gain the fabulous Golden Fleece, which had been guarded by a dragon. Medea and Jason had two sons, but eventually Jason fell in love with another woman. Medea was extremely upset and, although she dearly loved her children, she decided to kill them in order to hurt Jason.

In this extract from the play, Medea is lamenting the difficulties women face when they marry.

Of all the creatures that live and have the ability to think, we women are most unfortunate. First we must buy a husband with our dowry and then we must take him as our master. We must, for not to take a husband means still worse suffering. And the great question is whether we take a bad or a good husband. For it is not respectable for a woman to divorce, nor is she able to refuse a husband. If a woman learns how to treat her husband and he does not bear the yoke of marriage with reluctance, then she is enviable. If not, it is better to die. A bored husband can cheer himself up outside the home, but we may not. Men tell us that we live at home out of danger while they fight in war. How stupid! I would rather stand in the ranks three times than give birth to one child.

Euripides   *Medea*

Marriage as a Cure for Wildness!

Greek authors recognized that as girls grew up, they often became restless and difficult to please. Many (male) writers believed that the best method of curing this restlessness was to marry the girls off, because running a household and looking after children would keep them busy. Some authors also believed that marriage had beneficial effects on young men. Either their new responsibilities would encourage a troublesome young man to settle down, or his new wife would make him do so!

Making clothes and soft furnishings (such as rugs, blankets, bedcovers, cushions, and wall hangings) occupied a considerable amount of a woman's time. This was because she did not buy ready-made fabric, but had to produce her own cloth. Linen was sometimes used, but most fabric was woolen. To start with, a woman bought wool sheared from a sheep. This wool had to be cleaned, brushed, and spun into thread. Once the wool had been spun it was then set up on a weaving loom. Weaving required considerable skill and it

This woman is spinning wool onto a spindle to make thread, which can then be woven into cloth. Making clothes and furnishings, such as blankets, would have occupied much of a woman's time.

was an opportunity for women to display their creative talent by designing beautiful patterns and pictures.

As well as making cloth, women spent a lot of time looking after the house. Women were responsible for repairing furniture and for supervising the shopping for the household. They had to ensure that there were enough stores laid up for winter, and they may have salted their own fish and prepared their own dried fruit. Poorer women, who did not have household slaves, would have spent time fetching water from a spring or well. This was not necessarily an unpopular chore, as it took women outside the house and gave them the opportunity to meet and talk with other women. Richer women did not have this freedom, as they were not supposed to run the risk of meeting men who were not related to them. Rich women therefore tended to spend most of their time indoors in their own quarters.

Women were very busy and probably did not have much leisure time. There were several female poets who gained fame in antiquity, such as Sappho (*SAFF-oh*), but little of their writing has survived, and it is not known how often their work was read by women. Some vase paintings preserve pictures of women reading, but most women would not have been sufficiently educated to read with ease. Indeed, some men strongly disapproved of the idea of women being taught to read at all. One character in a comedy play stated that teaching women to read was a very bad idea, equivalent to giving extra poison to a venomous snake!

Women were not encouraged to take an interest in the male spheres of politics and government. However, the Greek philosopher, Plato, believed that there was nothing to prevent women from

Working Women

Although the Athenian ideal was of a modest woman who spent her time indoors weaving and looking after her children, this was not always the case. Poor women sometimes ran stalls in markets, selling ribbons, flowers, bread, and vegetables. Women also acted as midwives. Historians recorded that in early Athenian society women were not allowed to study or to practice medicine. However, one courageous woman called Hagnodike (*Hag-NOH-dik-eh*) was so determined to study medicine that she dressed up as a man in order to attend lectures. She maintained her disguise once she had been trained, and acted as a doctor to pregnant women. She was so successful that rival practitioners grew jealous and prosecuted her for gaining undue influence over her patients. Hagnodike was forced to reveal that she was a woman, and her accusers were even more determined to have her convicted of wrongful behavior. However, the women of Athens who had benefited from Hagnodike's care and attention supported her, and the law was changed to allow Athenian women to study medicine.

being involved in running the state, just because they were women. In his book called the *Republic* (dating to the 380s B.C.E.), Plato argued that those who were capable of being leaders, both men and women, ought to be trained for high office. This was an unusual attitude for his time. Plato also realized that it would be difficult to combine a career and motherhood. His solution was that women who were involved with governing the state must not be distracted from their leadership role by bringing up their children. Instead, the children should be handed over to state-run nurseries to be brought up by other women.

Women's Activities Outside the Home

Most of a woman's time was spent indoors, running her household. However, there were opportunities for women to get outside the house during festivals. These were not only religious occasions, but also times of celebration and enjoyment. Women took part either as ordinary worshippers or in a special role, such as that of priestess.

> ## Little Bears
>
> Certain young Athenian girls took part in an ancient ceremony at the Temple of Artemis at Brauron (*BROW-ron*). Many of the exact details of what happened are not known, but it appears that girls as young as nine lived in the sanctuary for a year carrying out various duties in the temple complex. They were known as *arktoi* (*ARK-toy*), or bears, and as well as their routine in the temple, they also ran in races and took part in bear dances. This ceremony was supposed to have originated when Artemis was angry because a young Athenian man had killed a bear, which was sacred to her. To make up for this bad act, every year girls had to work in her temple.

One of the most important festivals was the Panathenaia (*Pa-na-then-EYE-uh*), held in honor of Athena, the patron goddess of Athens. Every four years a larger version of the Panathenaia took place. This version was called the Great Panathenaia. At this festival a new robe was brought to the Parthenon and presented to the goddess. Women had many important roles within this ceremony. A select number of women wove the sacred robe. Some women carried it into the temple and presented it to the goddess, while other women acted as "basket bearers" in the procession and carried baskets containing sacred objects.

The Great Panathenaia was not the only festival where women had a major role. The Thesmophoria (*Thez-moe-FOE-ree-uh*) was a festival sacred to Demeter, the goddess of crops. It lasted for three days in the autumn and was only open to women. The ceremony was concerned with ensuring that the seed that was to be planted in the spring was fertile and would produce good crops. Women were thus associated with a very important part of the agricultural calendar. The festival was also one of the few times when citizen women could get away from their homes and families, and they spent the nights at the sanctuary in special huts built to house them during the festival.

Greek clothes were made from rectangular pieces of cloth tied at the waist. Sometimes a cloak would be worn on top of the basic tunic to provide extra warmth.

How Do We Know?

Most evidence for what the ancient Greeks wore and other aspects of their appearance, such as hairstyles, comes from art. Sculpture shows changes in hairstyles, but it is not very informative about male clothes, because Greek statues of men were naked. Vase painting is particularly useful for reflecting changing fashions in dress. It is detailed and gives a good idea of the rippling effect of the clothes the Greeks wore.

Clothes

Greek clothes were very simple, being made from rectangular pieces of cloth joined together. The basic garment was the tunic, which had holes for the head and arms. Young men and children wore short tunics that reached the knee. This gave the wearer plenty of freedom of movement so that they could run or move quickly. Women and older men wore longer tunics that covered their legs. Tunics were usually worn with a belt, which pulled the garment tight around the waist. There were two types of women's tunics. The *peplos* (*PEHP-loss*) was pinned at the shoulders and tied at the waist with a belt. It was made of wool and fell in quite stiff folds down to the feet. It seems that younger, unmarried women tended to wear the peplos, whereas older women wore a *chiton* (*KY-ton*). The chiton was made of lighter wool or linen, and fastened along the arms with buttons. It tended to cling to the body in rippling folds.

Cloaks were worn over a tunic, particularly in cold weather. The cloak, or *himation* (*hih-MAT-ee-on*), was basically a rectangular piece of cloth, which was draped over one shoulder and the opposite arm. Both men and women wore the himation, although unmarried women might also wear a shoulder mantle draped around both shoulders. Women might

This image from a Greek pot shows a woman sitting on a cushion as she puts on a pair of sandals. She wears a bracelet, earrings, and a necklace and has her hair piled up high on her head and held in place by a hairnet.

Hairstyles

Men wore their hair fairly short. In the Classical period, they usually had beards, but in the Hellenistic period (after 323 B.C.E.) they went clean-shaven. Hairstyles for women varied according to age. Young or unmarried women had long hair, which might be braided. Older, married women tended to wear their hair tied up under a hairnet. Women might also wear decoration in their hair, such as gold sprays in the shape of leaves. Some women wore wigs or dyed their hair to blonde or dark brown. In the Hellenistic period, women often put waves into their hair to ensure that it curled in a fashionable way. However, whatever style was in fashion, only slave women wore their hair cut short.

In Classical times, men wore their hair fairly short. Beards were still normal for men.

Early Greek vase painting suggests that long hair and beards were fashionable before the Classical period.

This young man is clean-shaven and has short hair. This sort of appearance became fashionable in the Hellenistic period.

This woman has tied her hair up with cloth. A hairnet or ribbons might also be used.

Young women tended to let their long hair hang down in braids or in waves. A ribbon might be used to keep hair off the face.

Coping with the Heat

In Greece, the weather is often very hot. Both men and women wore hats to protect them from the strong sunshine. These hats were usually made of straw or wool (they also had hats made of fur, for the colder weather). Women would carry fans to keep them cool in hot weather and both men and women used perfume, partly because running water was not available, and it was harder to wash regularly.

wear a himation made from a light, gauzy material in hot weather, or a warmer one made from wool when it was cold. While men often wore the himation, when they were riding they tended to use a shorter cloak, called a *chlamys* (*KLAH-miss*). This was fastened with a pin or brooch and allowed greater movement than a himation.

Clothes came in different colors. Red, yellow, green, black, and purple dyes were all used. Dyes were made from berries, onions, colored earth, and lichen. Purple dye was made from ground-up sea snails, known as murex. This dye had to be imported from the great trading city of Tyre (in Palestine) and was very expensive, so only the rich wore purple clothes. The very poorest people probably wore clothes that had not been dyed, but were simply the color of the natural wool. Linen was more expensive than wool, and the very wealthy might also buy clothes made from imported silk.

As well as being colored, cloth might have patterns of geometric shapes woven into the material. The borders of clothes could be decorated with scenes from mythology, or pictures of animals. Fashions in clothes also changed. During the Archaic period (before the fifth century B.C.E.), clothes were highly colored and brightly patterned. During the fifth century B.C.E., they tended to be made of one color, with only a small pattern or a strip of color at the edge. In the fourth century, patterned materials again became very popular. Such materials might be made even more elaborate by having gold decoration sewn onto the material.

Beauty

Just as today, women in ancient Greece liked to look attractive. A whole range of beauty aids have been found by archaeologists. Razors, scissors, combs, and brushes were used to keep hair neat, and ribbons, hairbands, slides, and hairpins could be added. Makeup was widely used and Greek women had access to blush, foundation, lipstick, rouge, eyeshadow, and false hair curls. A suntan was not considered attractive, so women tried to keep out of the sun. Some might also conceal a suntan with foundation made from white lead. However, this was potentially dangerous. Too much white lead could cause a rash or even poison a woman. Women could check their appearance in highly polished bronze mirrors. The final touch was jewelry, which consisted of necklaces, earrings, bracelets, and brooches. Richer women wore jewelry made from gold or silver, while that of poorer women was made of bronze, bone, iron, lead, or glass.

Footwear

The ancient Greeks tended to go barefoot indoors, or wear light slippers. Men and boys wore sandals outside the home, and, during cold weather, fur-lined boots. Women would also wear sandals if they went outdoors. If a woman wanted to appear taller than she actually was, she would wear shoes with special cork soles and high heels.

The ancient Greeks thought that a light complexion in women was attractive. This small storage vessel is made in the shape of a woman and probably contained oil or perfume.

Slavery

Slavery is a cruel institution. However, in the ancient world, it was common practice to own slaves. Some slaves would live with a family and do domestic work, while others would work for their owners in small businesses. The most demanding job was working in the mines, where dangerous conditions and hard physical work meant a life of toil and misery. Although the Greeks valued the concept of freedom highly, they tolerated a situation where other human beings were enslaved and bought and sold like cattle.

Where Did Slaves Come From?

Wars provided the most common source of slaves. Ancient societies were not bound by strict conventions as to how war was to be waged, and it was normal to enslave the inhabitants of captured cities. The money gained by selling captives was regarded as one of the perks of soldiers in a successful war. Not only foreigners, but also Greeks themselves could be sold into slavery after being captured. Some of these Greeks would have been lucky enough to be liberated by friends or relatives who found the money to buy their freedom, but not all could have been so fortunate.

The best evidence for slavery comes from Athens. By the fifth century B.C.E., the majority of slaves were not Greek, but came from the lands to the north and east of

Some female slaves had special skills, such as hairdressing or looking after children. However, most female slaves were bought to carry out lots of different household tasks, such as cleaning, cooking, serving food at dinner parties, and helping to make wool for clothes.

Enslavement Because of Debt

In the seventh century B.C.E., some Athenians faced a real danger of enslavement, not through war, but poverty. These Athenians were poor farmers who needed to borrow money to pay off existing debts, or buy corn seed to grow in the fields. When they borrowed money, they used their own bodies for security. If they did not repay the debt, the person to whom they owed money could seize them and sell them into slavery. Around 594 B.C.E., the great Athenian lawgiver, Solon (*SO-lon*), made it illegal to secure loans in this way, and for any Athenian to be enslaved at Athens. However, it is clear that by the time he made these laws, many Athenians had already suffered the fate of being enslaved for failing to pay back a debt. Solon himself wrote that he had to buy back Athenians who had been sold abroad.

The Athenian lawgiver, Solon, was shocked that Athenian citizens were being sold abroad as slaves because they had fallen into debt. Solon banned the practice and rescued some Athenians from slavery.

Greece. Some of these slaves had been captured by pirates, but certain areas, such as Thrace (northeast of Greece), supplied large numbers of slaves for the Greek market. These slaves might have been prisoners captured in local wars, or simply unimportant people, powerless to prevent their enslavement. Men, women, and children were all supplied for sale, and Greek authors recorded that Thracian (*THRAY-shun*) parents sometimes sold their own children into slavery. Children born to slave parents were automatically slaves themselves. Other children might become slaves even though they had been born to free parents. Children abandoned at birth, found and adopted, were normally brought up as slaves.

Ancient authors are not reliable when it comes to numbers, and it is very difficult to come to an accurate assessment of how many slaves there actually were in Athens. It seems that, in the fifth century B.C.E., perhaps between one quarter and one third of the Athenian population were slaves.

Work

Slaves worked in a number of capacities in Greece, ranging from general agricultural or domestic chores to specialist trades. In agriculture, slaves would have carried out many different tasks, such as plowing, tying up vines, collecting the olive harvest, or clearing the fields of stones. Doubtless these slaves were made to work harder than their masters, but the type of work would have been very similar to that of a normal peasant farmer. However, a much harsher life was faced by those slaves who were sent to work in the mines.

Mining

Silver had been mined from the region of Laurion (*LAU-ree-on*), in the south of Attica, since the sixteenth century B.C.E. However, mining expanded greatly after a rich seam of silver was found in the 480s B.C.E. As many as 20,000 slaves were used in silver mining, both underground, cutting away the rock, and above ground, extracting the silver. Mining was a labor-intensive process that required much energy and organization. By the time organized mining ended in 102 B.C.E., the region of Laurion was pitted with around 2,000 shafts connecting over 80 miles (130 kilometers) of tunnels. One tunnel was over 1 mile (1.6 kilometers) long.

Slaves who worked underground faced ten-hour shifts in dangerous conditions. Entry into the mine was down a deep, narrow mineshaft measuring 6 feet (2 meters) by 4 feet (1.3 meters) and reaching a depth of up to 360 feet (110 meters). Very narrow tunnels about 3 feet (1 meter) square ran off the main shaft, and slaves crawled along these to reach the rock face being worked. They used chisels and hammers to cut away the rock, which was then dragged up to the surface where the silver would be extracted. This was exhausting work—slaves spent hours kneeling or lying down, hacking away at the rock face by the light of a small oil lamp. Mining was also dangerous. There was an ever-present threat that the air supply might become contaminated, or that a tunnel might collapse. Moreover, the risk of collapse was actually increased by some unscrupulous mine contractors. When the tunnels were dug out, pillars of the original rock were left to provide support. However, some contractors removed these pillars to get the silver ore they contained, even though doing this considerably increased the chance that the roof of the tunnel might cave in.

Once on the surface, the chunks of rock were ground up and then washed in special washeries to get rid of any sediment. The remainder was heated to a high temperature and smelted to separate any lead in the rock from the silver. The removal of the lead left pure silver, to be used in a variety of ways, including making the fine silver currency, decorated with an owl, for which Athens was famous.

Trade and Business

If a slave was skilled in a trade, he was often able to use his expertise, despite not being a free man. Some slaves worked and lived alongside their master, helping him in his business. If a

Mining was exhausting work, and slaves who were sent to the mines had very little chance of ever regaining their freedom.

Renting Out a Silver Mine

The Athenian silver mines were owned by the state, but leased out to private contractors who organized the excavation of the silver ore. These contractors might be citizens or metics (resident foreigners), and they undertook to pay a certain sum to the state for the right to mine silver for three or more years. Slaves were often hired in large numbers to work in the mines—the Athenian general, Nicias (*NICK-ee-ass*), owned 1,000 slaves who he hired out to mine contractors. The contractors were responsible for providing all food and replacing any slaves who died, and Nicias made a lot of money from providing slaves, without having to organize any actual digging.

master owned a large business, then the slaves might work in something resembling a factory. There was one workshop that made armor and was staffed with 120 slaves, and a knife maker with 32 men. However, most workshops were probably much smaller and run directly by a craftsman-owner.

Some slaves were bought as an investment. When this happened, the owner planned to earn money from the slave's work, rather than using the slave to help him in his own business. The owner would either hire out the slave or set him up in business. The slave would give the majority of his earnings to his master, but would be allowed to keep a certain proportion. Such slaves often did not live with their owner, and had some degree of independence. They also had the opportunity to save up in order to buy their freedom.

Citizens and slaves often worked together. Sometimes this was because the slave was operating alongside his master in his workshop, but both free men and slaves were employed on some of the great public works at Athens. For example, when the Erechtheum was built on the Acropolis of Athens, a detailed list of costs was kept. These building accounts record what each workman was paid and what job he did. Of the 71 workers employed, 20 were citizens, 35 were metics, and 16 were slaves. All were paid the same wage for the same job, no matter whether they were slaves or free men. Slaves could also rise to a position of responsibility, just as citizens did. The Erechtheum accounts show that there were six foremen employed to oversee the building work. Three of the foremen were citizens, two were metics, but one was a slave.

Domestic Slaves

Slaves who lived in homes would carry out a variety of domestic chores. Most households would have had one or two all-purpose slaves, and specialist slaves, such as hairdressers or tutors, were probably only employed in the richest households. However, while rich Romans often had hundreds of slaves working in their houses, this number did not exist in the homes of rich Greeks. It seems likely that even a rich household would have had a maximum of

What Sort of Trades Did Slaves Work In?

Slaves worked in a huge number of different industries. They were goldsmiths, bronze workers, shield makers, potters, cobblers, shoemakers, carpenters, fabric makers, lyre makers, bankers, architects, doctors, and teachers. There were even certain public slaves who were owned by the Athenian state.

Some of these slaves carried out ordinary roles such as road building or street cleaning. Others were used to guard prisoners and carry out executions. There were also ten temple repairers at the sanctuary of Eleusis, and slaves with the responsible role of clerks or keepers of the city archive.

This illustration, taken from a Greek vase, shows a number of people busy in a bronze workshop. The two clothed men are customers or a customer and the owner. The smaller figures of men working on the statue of the warrior are slaves. In art, slaves were often shown as small figures in order to signify their humble status.

around twenty resident slaves. If a Greek owned more slaves than this he would have used them in business or hired them out to others, rather than employing them in his household.

Female slaves often did domestic work. Some would serve as maids, doing the cooking and cleaning, or fetching water from streams and wells. They would also serve food at dinner parties and tidy up afterward. Others would look after the children of the house or help their mistress to put on her clothes and makeup, and arrange her hair in the latest fashionable style. One very important role was to help make clothes. Greek clothes were woven by hand and slave girls would help to spin the wool and weave the cloth. Manumission lists (lists showing who was freed from slavery) have survived from classical Athens and the most common occupation listed for freed female slaves is that of wool worker.

Citizen women were not allowed to mix with men who were not part of their family, so they did not attend dinner parties. However, many Greek men enjoyed the company of women, and slave girls were often brought to dinner parties to provide entertainment. Some were there to provide conversation, but most were dancing girls or musicians who sang and played the flute. Also, female acrobats could be hired to entertain guests at dinner parties. Male slaves were also used in domestic roles. Men were useful as household overseers, porters, or doorkeepers, and some rich Greeks had bodyguards who accompanied them when they went outside.

Pasion—A Very Successful Slave

One man called Pasion (*PAH-see-on*) not only managed to buy his freedom, but was a very successful businessman in his own right. Pasion was born around 430 B.C.E., perhaps in Phoenecia, the great trading nation of the Middle East. There is no evidence as to when or why he became enslaved, but at some point before 400 B.C.E. he was brought to Athens, where he was put to work for two Athenian bankers.

Pasion worked hard and it was not long before he had earned the trust of his two masters. He was given his freedom in the early fourth century, and by 394 B.C.E he appears to have become the owner of the bank. He proceeded to make a fortune as a banker and was extremely rich when he died in 370 B.C.E. However, Pasion did not keep his money just for himself and his family. He also made impressive gifts to the Athenian state—he provided 1,000 shields and paid for the building of five *triremes* (warships), and provided the pay for their crews. It was very costly to provide these ships, but Pasion also lent the Athenian state further large sums of money to help finance the Athenian fleet.

The Athenians recognized Pasion's generosity and granted him a reward—he and his two sons were made citizens. However, this grant of citizenship was exceptional, and most slaves would have lived out their whole lives without any chance of freedom.

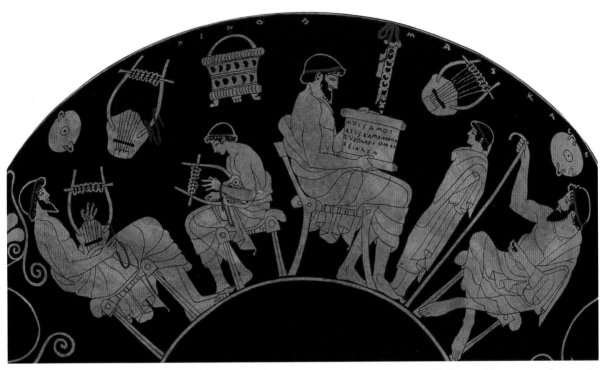

When Greek boys went to school they were accompanied by a slave called a *paidogogus*, who made sure that they behaved properly. The man sitting on the far right holding a stick is probably a paidogogus.

Treatment of Slaves

How well slaves were treated depended partly on the job the slave was doing. A slave girl who looked after the mistress of the house was likely to be given much better food and clothing than a man working underground in the mines. Skilled slaves also tended to be better treated, because they cost more money than unskilled slaves and were harder to replace. Some slaves were considered to be very much part of the family and were treated kindly, but they still did not have freedom and were dependent on the kindness of their owner. If their owner died, they might be handed over to someone who did not know them and had little interest in their happiness. Slaves who were set up in business had more independence than others, but they were still considered to be decidedly inferior beings.

Slaves had no legal rights. They could not legally own anything and they had no right to marry. The low status of slaves was underlined by the fact that they could not give evidence in court unless it had been extracted under torture. Slaves were believed to be naturally inclined to lie and it was thought that they would only tell the truth when tortured. In fact, torture made a slave's evidence less reliable, but the law was not changed. It was considered acceptable to punish slaves by beating or whipping them, although it was illegal to kill them.

The Helots

Most evidence for slavery comes from Athens. Slavery existed in other Greek states but, in Sparta, slavery took an unusual form. In the eighth century B.C.E., the Spartans had invaded the fertile region of Messenia (*Mess-EE-nee-uh*), which lay to the west of Sparta. They conquered the Messenians and enslaved them. However, the Messenian slaves, known as Helots, were not given to individual Spartans; they were owned by the Spartan state itself. Helots could not be set free, killed, or moved from one estate to another without the specific order of the state. Their main job was as agricultural workers, to produce food for their Spartan rulers. However, the male Helots might also be ordered to fight as lightly armed troops for the Spartans. Sometimes these men might be freed if they fought very bravely, but it seems that this was a rare reward.

This image from a Greek pot shows a slave busily carrying large storage jars.

Not all male slaves carried out physical work. Some educated slaves taught children how to read or to play music.

The Helots resented their role as slaves, and the Spartans feared that they might rebel, destroying the privileged Spartan way of life. Although the evidence is not entirely clear, it seems that the Spartans did everything that they could to keep the Helots too scared to revolt. One method was the *krypteia* (*KROOP-tay-ah*). This was a secret operation which was carried out at night. Young Spartans would be sent out to roam around the countryside, armed only with daggers, to kill any Helots they met. Specific Helots who were suspected of being potentially dangerous were also hunted down and killed. This exercise was doubly useful for the Spartan state. It not only allowed useful military training in night operations to take place, but it was also a highly effective method of striking fear into the Helots.

However, the Spartan system did not last. The numbers of true Spartan citizens declined, and eventually Sparta's power was challenged by the state of Thebes. When a Theban army invaded Sparta in the 370s B.C.E., the Messenians revolted and regained their freedom.

A Law to Protect Slaves?

In Athens it was illegal to hit slaves in the street. Some Athenians complained about this and argued that slaves ought not be protected in this way. However, one Athenian writer argued that the law had been introduced not to protect slaves, but to protect poor Athenian citizens! He argued that it was impossible to tell free men from slaves in the streets because some slaves dressed in rich clothes, but some citizens were poorly dressed. Therefore, the law ensured that nobody would strike a citizen because he had mistaken him for a slave. The argument is almost certainly an exaggeration, but it does show that some slaves might be better looked after than some of the very poorest Athenians who struggled to make a living.

Slaves and citizens worked together on some of the great building projects at Athens, including the Erechtheum, left.

Slaves were paid the same rate as free citizens and some were even placed in positions of authority. Here a slave and a citizen move blocks of stone into place with levers—a physically demanding and skilled job.

Greek Society in Action

In many ways, Greek society appears today to be contradictory. Greeks believed passionately in their own freedom, yet they accepted the concept of slavery. The Athenians were very proud of their democracy, which allowed every male citizen, no matter how poor or unimportant, the right to vote on vital decisions. In contrast, Athenian citizen women had little freedom of independent action and were heavily dependent upon their male relatives. Spartans believed that they were the freest of the Greeks because they did not have to take part in trade or work for a living. However, they were brought up under an extremely rigorous regime where the individual had little personal freedom and there was no room for those who did not conform or succeed.

However, historical societies cannot be judged by modern standards. For example, today's society disapproves of the evil of slavery, but the fact that slavery was normal in Greek times does not mean that we should dismiss everything that the Greeks achieved. No society is perfect, but we can learn from the past; what matters most about the Greek world was what it gave to later generations in fields such as art, architecture, literature, philosophy, history, science, politics, and democracy.

Athenian coins carried the image of an owl, the symbol of Athena. The silver for these coins came from the silver mines at Laurion, which were worked by slaves.

The Bravest of the Helots Disappear

The historian Thucydides records that during the Peloponnesian War between Athens and Sparta (431–404 B.C.E.), the Spartans were so afraid the Helots might take the opportunity to launch a rebellion that they put together a ruthless plan. They said that they were going to free those Helots who had fought best for the Spartans in the recent war, and told the Helots to decide who were the best fighters. Two thousand Helots were chosen, and they went around the sanctuaries with garlands on their heads as if they had been set free. However, shortly afterward they disappeared and nobody could discover what had happened to them. The Spartans had secretly killed them, believing that the men who had fought most effectively in battle were the ones whose boldness and daring they most had to fear.

Glossary

agora marketplace

agricultural relating to farming

arable relating to growing crops

arktoi Athenian girls taking part in a special "little bears" ceremony at the Temple of Artemis

aulos a wind instrument, rather like a double flute

bier a funeral table

boule Athenian democratic council of 500 men selected by lottery

chiton a light woollen or linen tunic

chlamys a cloak, shorter than the himation

crotala castanets

democracy government by the people, or the majority

dikasteria law courts in the Athenian democracy

dowry money or property that a woman brings to her husband on marriage

ecclesia Athenian democratic assembly of male citizens which discussed political matters

ephebe young man doing his military training

Ephor one of five magistrates elected each year in Sparta

export to sell or trade goods outside the region

Gerousia a council of elders who advised the kings of Sparta

grammatistes teacher of reading and writing

gymnasia training grounds

Helot slave of Sparta

Heraia athletic festival for girls, held in honor of Hera

himation a simple cloak

import to buy in goods from outside the region

keras a musical instrument like a curved horn

kithara wooden musical instrument, rather like a large lyre

kitharistes music teacher

kymbala cymbals

lichen a combination of algae, or simple plants, and fungus

loutrophoros a tall vase with long handles

lyre stringed musical instrument

manumission the act of freeing a slave

metics foreign residents in Athens

murex a purple dye made from sea snails

obol a small coin placed in the mouths of the dead to pay the fee for crossing the Styx River

oligarchy government by a few people

ostracism an event in which the ecclesia selected a man to be sent into exile for ten years

paidogogus a slave who escorted boys to school

paidotribes athletics teacher

palaestra a building where boys would learn how to wrestle

pankration a particularly violent form of wrestling

peplos a woollen tunic

revenue income, or earnings

rhetor teacher of rhetoric

rhetoric the art of public speaking

salpinx a kind of trumpet

sambuca a type of harp

sarcophagus a stone coffin

stele a raised stone slab, often used to mark a grave

Styx river which separated the Underworld from Earth

symposium an entertaining discussion at a dinner party

syrinx a set of pipes

trireme a warship

truce an agreed time of peace

tympana a kind of tambourine

urban relating to towns or cities

Glossary of Names

Alcibiades a rich Athenian politician

Apollo God of the sun, father of Asclepius

Aristogeiton one of the killers of Hipparchus; honored by the Athenians for having ended tyranny in Athens

Artemis goddess of hunting and the moon, sister of Apollo

Asclepius god of medicine, son of Apollo

Athena goddess of war, arts and crafts, and wisdom

Charon the man who ferried the souls of the dead across the Styx River to the Underworld

Cypselus the first Greek tyrant at Corinth

Dionysus god of wine and drama

Euripides Athenian dramatist

Hades god of the Underworld

Hagnodike an Athenian woman who pretended to be a man in order to study medicine

Harmodius one of the killers of Hipparchus; honored by the Athenians for having ended tyranny in Athens

Hera wife of Zeus

Hermes messenger of the gods, son of Zeus and Maia

Herodotus Greek historian

Hipparchus brother of Hippias, the tyrant of Athens

Hippias son of Pisistratus and tyrant at Athens

Hippocrates a fifth-century B.C.E. doctor, honored as the Father of Medicine

Jason leader of the Argonauts

Medea daughter of Aeetes, brother of Absyrtus, said to be a witch

Nicias Athenian general

Pasion a slave who bought his freedom

Pisistratus tyrant of Athens

Polycrates tyrant of the island of Samos

Sappho female poet

Solon great sixth-century Athenian lawgiver

Thucydides historian

Learn More About

Books

Biesty, Stephen. *Greece in Spectacular Cross-Section.* Oxford: Oxford University Press, 2006.

Chrisp, Peter. *A Greek Theater* (Look Inside series). Austin, Texas: Raintree Steck-Vaugh, 2000.

Chrisp, Peter. *Ancient Greece Revealed.* New York: Dorling Kindersley, 2003.

Hynson, Colin. *Ancient Greece.* Milwaukee, Wisconsin: Gareth Stevens, 2005.

Millard, Anne. *Family Life in Ancient Greece.* London: Hodder & Stoughton, 2001.

Ross, Stewart. *Ancient Greece—Daily Life.* Mankato, Minnesota: Compass Point Books, 2007.

Ross, Stewart. *Ancient Greece—History in Stone.* San Diego, California: Silver Dolphin, 2002.

Ross, Stewart. *Ancient Greece—Tales of the Dead.* New York: Dorling Kindersley, 2004.

Tames, Richard. *People in the Past—Ancient Greek Children.* Chicago, Illinois: Heinemann Library, 2003.

Woff, Richard. *The Ancient Greek Olympics.* New York: Oxford University Press, 2000.

Web Sites

Acropolis 360-degree Tour
www.acropolis360.com

British Museum—Ancient Greece
www.ancient-greece.co.uk

Daily Life in Ancient Greece
http://members.aol.com/Donnclass/Greeklife.html

Greece Museums
www.ancient-greece.org/museum.html

HistoryWiz—Ancient Greece
www.historywiz.com/anc-greece.htm

National Archaeological Museum of Athens
www.culture.gr/2/21/214/21405m/e21405m1.html

TeacherOz—Greeks
www.teacheroz.com/greeks.html

The Ancient City of Athens
www.stoa.org/athens

University of Pennsylvania—The Ancient Greek World
www.museum.upenn.edu/Greek_World/index.html

University of Richmond—Voyage Back in Time, Ancient Greece and Rome
http://oncampus.richmond.edu/academics/education/projects/webunits/greecerome/index.html

World News Network—Ancient Greece
www.ancientgreece.com

Index

Page numbers in *italics* refer to images and captions

adoption 54
agora 20–21
Alcibiades 28
Amasis 11
Apollo 30
Archaic Period 62
aristocrats 9–10, 13
Aristogeiton *12*
Asclepius *30*, 31, *32–33*
Athena 58, 75
Athens:
  Acropolis *16–17*
  adoption 54
  aristocrats 13
  citizenship 10
  debt 66
  democracy 14
  Empire 14–15
  gymnasium 44
  imports and exports 21–22
  Parthenon *17*
  slavery 66, 74
  tyranny 13

babies and infants *36*, 37–38
beauty 62, *63*
boule 14

Cerberus 35
chariot racing 28
Charon *31*, 34
childhood *36*, 37–38, *38*, *39*,
  40, 41, 42, *42*, 43, *43*, 44, *44*,
  45, 46–49, *46*, *47*, *49*, 65, 66
China 21

chlamys 62
citizenship 10
clothes 54, 55–58, *56*, *59*, 60,
  60
Corinth 10
Cypselus 10

death and funerals 31, *31*,
  34–35, *34–35*
debt 66
Delian League 15
Delos 15
Delphi 27
democracy 10
dikasteria 14
Dionysus *22*
divorce 53
domestic life *50*, 51–63, *52*,
  54, *56*, *59*, *60*, *61*, *63*

ecclesia 14
education *36*, 37–49, *38*, *39*,
  42, *43*, *44*, *45*, *46*, *47*, *49*
Egypt 11, 21
Eleusis 69
Ephebes 47
Ephors 13–14
Epidauros 31, *33*
Erechtheum 69
Euripides 55

farming 19–20, *20*
fishing 21, *21*
footwear 63
forms of government 9–17,
  11, *12*, *13*, *16–17*
fox and the boy, the 49

gerousia 14
girls:
  education for 46, *46*, 48
  Spartan 48
Golden Fleece 55
gymnasium 44

Hagnodike *57*
hairstyles 61, *61*
Harmodius *12*
Hellenistic Period 61
Helots 10, 72, 73, 75
Hera 26
Heraia 26
Hermes 34
Herodotus 11
himation 60
Hippias 13
Hippocrates 31
home 55–58

imports and exports 21–22
Isthmian Games 27

krypteia 73

language 52
Laurion 67

marketplace 20–21
marriage 52–55, *54*
meals and dinner parties 23,
  23
Medea 55
medicine and illness 28, *29*,
  30–31, *30*, *32–33*
Messenia 72
metics 10

military service 47, *47*
mining 67
monarchy 9, 13
music 42, *42*, 43, *43*

Nemean Games 27

oligarchy 10, 13
olive oil 19, 21, 23
Olympic Games 25–28
ostracism 15

Paidogogus *71*
palaestra 44
Panathenaia 58
Panhellenic Games 27
Pankration 27
Pasion 70
pastimes and ceremonies *24*,
    *25–35, 26, 27, 29, 30, 31,
    32–33, 34–35*
Peloponnesian War 28
Peplos 60
Persia 14, 16
Persian Wars 15, 16

Pisistratus 12, 13
Plato 57–58
Polycrates 11
pottery 21
public speaking 46–47
Pythian Games 27

reading and writing 40, 41, 42
Republic (Plato) 58

Samos 11, *11*
Sappho 57
Sardis 11
Segesta, Sicily *8*
slavery *64*, 65–75
Solon 66
Sparta:
    growing up in 48–49
    oligarchy 10, 13
    ruins *13*
    slavery 72, 73, 75
    war with Athens 75
sport and athletics *24*, 25–35,
    *26, 27, 29, 30, 31, 32–33,
    34–35*, 44, 46

Styx River *31*, 34, 35

tax 22
Thebes 73
Thesmophoria 58
Thessaly 19
Tholos *32*
Thrace 66
Thucydides 75
trade and commerce *18*,
    19–23, *20, 21, 22, 23*, 67–68
travel 22–23, *22*
tyranny 10, 12, 13
Tyre 62

Underworld *31*, 34, 35

women *50*, 51–63, *52, 54, 56,
    59, 60, 61, 63*